A Boy in the City

Poems by
Michael Miller

BLUE LIGHT PRESS ✦ 1ST WORLD PUBLISHING

1ST WORLD
PUBLISHING

SAN FRANCISCO ✦ FAIRFIELD ✦ DELHI

A Boy In The City

Copyright ©2021 Michael Miller

BLUE LIGHT PRESS
www.bluelightpress.com
bluelightpress@aol.com

1ST WORLD PUBLISHING
PO Box 2211
Fairfield, IA 52556
www.1stworldpublishing.com

BOOK & COVER DESIGN
Melanie Gendron
melaniegendron999@gmail.com

COVER PHOTO
Brooklyn Bridge, in the public domain

FIRST EDITION

ISBN: 978-1-4218-3709-3

For Wally Swist

I

Shame was Father leaving us,
Cruelty the boy shouting it
To everyone, "Miller has no Father!"
And anger found a breeding ground
Inside me. I imagined my fist
Striking out, my enemy silenced,
His bloody nose
A smear of retribution.

II

Mother was a bookkeeper
At Macy's, a hurrying woman
Sometimes leaving without a kiss.
At night she read Ellery Queen,
Crushed each Chesterfield
In a glass ashtray,
Drifted toward sleep
In a large bed
With emptiness beside her.
I knew nothing of burdens,
The stigma of divorce in 1947.

III

With her blonde hair
Wrapped in curlers
Mother was transformed.
I wanted Mother
Beautiful again,
Combing her hair
In the sunlight
Falling through the window.
I wanted to tiptoe
Into her room on Sunday morning
And slip into her warm bed
As she turned away,
Her hair a golden
Waterfall before me.
I was happy in the space
That Father had left.

IV

The large cannon
Before the Soldiers
And Sailors Monument
On Riverside Drive
Pointed at me.
I ran my small hand
Along the black barrel.
Did death wait to burst out
Of its wide mouth?
Every night I kept
The bedroom door opened,
The light on in the hall.

V

Riverside Park became
My sanctuary,
The trees my friends;
Maple, cherry, and sycamore
Welcomed me with
The whisper of leaves,
The silence of trunks.
I climbed to the top
Of the rocks,
My scraped knee
A badge of honor,
Then spread my arms
Toward the sky,
Lifting me out of myself.

VI

When I was old enough
To be left alone
And Grandmother went
To the hairdresser
I opened her drawer
And took out the corset,
A pale shade of pink.
Fitting it around
My chubby body
I pushed the long laces
Through the small eyes
And pulled them tight,
Winding them around the hooks.
I was going to be slim,
A pleasing shape in the mirror,
But I couldn't breathe,
I might die!
I ripped the corset off.

VII

Books became my friends,
My door opened wide
To a different world,
To Long John Silver,
The family Robinson,
The Mad Hatter.
I read beneath the covers
With my silver flashlight,
Every book calling out to me.
I stacked them neatly
On my table, wanting
A bookcase for my birthday.

VIII

In the Central Park Zoo
The polar bear
Bounded down the rocks,
Circled the cage,
Pressed its head
Against the bars.
Eyes looking out.
Standing before it
I belonged inside the bear,
Moving with its bulk,
Its grace,
Seeking a world.

IX

She was not supposed to die
From a ruptured appendix
In a room at Doctor's Hospital
Facing the East River.
Mother was supposed
To walk with me beside
The ongoing Hudson.
Each night before sleep
I felt my right side,
Touched it gently,
Asked God to keep
My appendix whole.

X

Roaring through the tunnel
Past an emerald eye
The express gathered speed,
A headstrong rush
Through darkness
Into the next station's
Waiting light.
I stood in the first car
Staring out the window;
One light led to another,
The speed winding down
At the amber, the red ahead.
I dreaded the end of the line,
The desolate station,
The long wait
For the return trip.

XI

I collected unbreakable objects:
Beautiful stones, railroad spikes,
Hubcaps that spun toward
Their own destination.
I placed them on my bookcase,
On the windowsill,
Holding them with regularity,
Beginning to love
Their permanence.

XII

In the gutted tenement
Boarded windows kept out
The light; bottles, needles,
Paper bags littered the floor,
The signatures of derelict lives.
I gripped my flashlight tighter,
Each uncertain step led me
Into rooms without doors,
Past rusty pipes
And rats hurrying away.
Without a friend beside me
An insistent voice
Told me to move forward,
To keep going —
I am still listening
To that voice.

XIII

To celebrate my thirteenth birthday
I walked across the Brooklyn Bridge
Above a sparkling river
Where a tugboat blasted its horn
And an explosion of gulls
Lifted my spirit
On a scattering of wings.
I stopped in the center
Of the bridge, its cables
The links of consistency,
Its curvature a graft
Of the eternal.

XIV

With riveting attention
I watched the soldiers marching
In the Armistice Day Parade
On Riverside Drive,
Their tan uniforms pressed
To perfection, their rifles
Pointing skyward,
Their steps in unison.
Too young to consider
The dead, the maimed,
I wanted to march among them.

XV

On the first day of school
In the noisy cafeteria
I sought my secret love.
"Where's Joanna?" I asked.
"She's dead," her friend replied,
"She died over the summer."
I wanted to speak,
I tried to speak,
The words were
Caught in my throat.

XVI

In my new notebook
On a blue-lined page
I tried to express my feelings;
I could only write,
"Joanna died, she was fourteen,"
My small, neat cursive
Containing a universe.
In my seventy-ninth spring
As the forsythia blooms
I am still trying
To write about Joanna.

XVII

Was I the grizzled fisherman
Or the glistening eel
He lifted out of the river?
I imagined the hook
In my mouth,
The air my enemy.
Laying the eel on the pier
The fisherman said,
"Pick it up, son.
Don't be afraid."
No one had ever called me son.
I moved, I bent quickly
And grabbed the eel,
This snake of the river,
This master of twists
That almost slithered
Through my hands.
But I would not let go,
I have never let go.

About the Author

Michael Miller's poems have appeared in *The Kenyon Review, The Sewanee Review, The Southern Review, Raritan, The Yale Review,* and other journals and books.

He lives in Amherst, Massachusetts.

www.ingramcontent.com/pod-product-compliance
Lightning Source LLC
Chambersburg PA
CBHW021918040426
42447CB00007B/917